WAVERLY SONGS II:
Time, Timing, Change

WAVERLY SONGS II:
Time, Timing, Change

Poetry by
ROBERT SONKOWSKY

iUniverse LLC
Bloomington

WAVERLY SONGS II: TIME, TIMING, CHANGE
Poetry by Robert Sonkowsky

iUniverse books may be ordered through booksellers or by contacting:

iUniverse LLC
1663 Liberty Drive
Bloomington, IN 47403
www.iuniverse.com
1-800-Authors (1-800-288-4677)

ISBN: 978-1-4759-9525-1 (sc)
ISBN: 978-1-4759-9526-8 (e)

Printed in the United States of America

iUniverse rev. date: 10/03/2013

Artwork credit: Al Thiemich

Contents

Dear Reader,

"Waverly" refers to the wonderful retirement village where I live, "Waverly Gardens" and to its other meaning, "wavering" or "quaking," as explained on the cover.

The photo of a nebula, superimposed in the center of the Quaking Aspen leaves on the front cover indicates the intent of the poems to reach out into the universe.

Foreword

Praise by fellow poets for a poem "Dismanteling Our Christmas Tree"—

peninsulapoet:
I like how the poem turns at the end to be a comment on mortality. Plus, the poem has a charming music.
Posted 01/14/2013 09:32 AM

Larry Schug:
This poem is a great example of how huge the "little" moments really are and if one is thoughtful, can draw life lessons from them. We should all know there are really no "little" moments in life. Thanks, Robert. Good work.
Posted 01/14/2013 08:12 AM

Praise by fellow poets for *"Feast from a Worker's Lunch Pail on a Hot Summer's Day"*—

Havenwood:
Delicious piece!
Posted 07/16/2013 08:39 AM

mimi:
yum
Posted 07/16/2013 08:27 AM

Preface

Introduction to Waverly Songs II:
Time, Timing, Change

As I have grown older, I have not necessarily grown wiser, at least not in brain-power, but I think my *heart* has grown more willing to communicate its thoughts to other hearts.

The word "Waverly" not only connotes the wonderful natural surroundings of Waverly Gardens, where I live with my wife, but also means "wavering/quaking" like the Quaking Aspen leaves on the cover of this book and like *me myself*: my hands shake because of my mild "familial tremor," and my general attitude and approach to life and to God shakes and quakes in ways that the poems in this second volume will develop.

Its subtitle *"Time, Timing, Change"* is intended to indicate, oxymoronically enough, a broad focus that includes age and aging but goes far beyond that into a whole universe both mundane and spiritual: the intervals and rhythms of Time and his polar servants love and death, birth and re-birth, memory of the past and faith in the future. My poems are in various forms—free verse, the sonnet, the villanelle *etc.*; I sometimes break the rules of form for our English adaptation of the Japanese Haiku and Tanka, in the orthodox version of which, rhyme is expressly forbidden, whereas I, the heretic, rhyme.

My poems sometimes speak for me myself personally, especially when they touch religion or politics, but more often the voice in the poem is *not* mine: "The truest poetry is the most feigning," says Auden. Our lives and our imaginations would be very limited and boring if we did not extend them to inhabit other *personae*. For example, I personally would not use the passé, male-chauvinist-pig expression "Hot Babe" as in one of my poems, nor view high heels as more attractive than, say, flip-flops or barefoot.

Yet all of my poems *do* come from my heart, intended for all human beings, young and old, whose hearts are open. If you are a parent, you may wish to shield kids you think too young for "Coochi Coo" and "A Twisted Brassiere Strap." Otherwise, please enjoy!

Myths of Time, Omitting Gory Details

The father of Zeus is Cronus/Kronos,
King in the Golden Age.
The Romans reincarnated Cronus
as Saturnus, ancient Italian god
of seeding and planting time,
pictured today as Father Time
carrying a scythe and perhaps a clock,
celebrated then in his Festival
of the Saturnalia, an optimistic time
of new growth, today an even more optimistic
time of gift-giving and the birthday
of the Christian god Jesus Christ.

Hysteron Proteron[*]

It would seem more right to me
if we could start out old
and grow down
young.
For now,
in backward line
with fresh youth first,
though not yet wise, we must choose our lives.

---

[*] Originally a Greek expression similar to 'the cart before the horse.'

You an' Me be Lovin' Fo'evah Now [sonnet]

"You an' me be lovin fo'evah now
cuz God gone hold our souls eternally,
nevah sleeps; home-boy, home-girl, we don' know;
home-boss neither; us immediately

wake: dang, where time gone? Was I stewed or cracked?
Seems like eternity passed, silent, hoo-ee!
How we be not zombies?" "We be black-backed.
Where's them there whites? Huh. Why ain them there free?"

"Honey-love, you hung up on trespass forgived?
Ain you, man, gone still be my girl, my girl?
One instant? Start over? Not long we lived
'gainst masks! Sides, man, no sin give love a whirl.

We this new world everthang everwhere
is love, we is love, not black, not white, bare."

Ars Poetica for Shaky Times
(Apologies to MaLeish and Horace*)

This little poem is in sonnet form;
a poet will need support from the past:
the best way to find it will be at last
to compose within a poetic norm :

limited available words will swarm
to the surface and will leave you aghast—
the poverty of English is unjust!
Though today we think slant rhymes do no harm.

In spite of which, here poets can wrestle
with their predecessors, while tradition
conjoins those on the same expedition,
same genre, in the same sacred vessel

of holy poetry, and hold support
in match after match with every effort.

---

*   Both the ancient Roman poet Horace and the modern poet Archibald Macleish wrote poems
titled *Ars Poetica* ('The Art of Poetry').

A Little Boy and His Dad Went Camping

A little boy and his dad went camping.
The boy was seven, his dad thirty-four.
A long hike and tent-up found them napping
in summer-time ease on the soft tent floor,
the little boy's head on his daddy's chest:
he liked the rumbling of his daddy's voice
soothing him, as a storm brewed in the west.
Thunder; lightening; rain deluged, left no choice,
as water rose on the floor of the tent,
but to fold, break camp, run fast to the car
hand-in-hand, store gear, sit wet-to-the-bone,
shivering—the ride home would not be far,
but a night like this years ago
had left them alone
and bereft, when a truck skidded and smashed
their passenger side where mother and wife
had been seated, leaving her body so gashed
boy and man, though dazed, remembered for life,
after their own hospitalization,
an image so stark now in the car that it paralyzed both—
with realization
in memory that made boy and man loath
to drive anywhere on any journey.
Nevertheless they set out and drove home,
image of beloved on a gurney
left in the past, went forward with my poem,
which ends with God's blessing, new family,
protected by loving old memory.

A Great-Grandfather
To His Baby Great-Granddaughter

We both take many naps,
your little cheek on my shoulder;
our eyes close and, perhaps,
we dream together, growing bolder
as I cuddle you closer,
warmer, as we slide through spangles
of sunbeams streaming
over thousands of wings of tiny angels
affecting our sleep with a purring,
a blinking and a nod.
Though asleep, we see a blurring,
a figure—is it God?
But down and down we go,
into a starry world,
round and round we go,
as if our dream had hurled
us into the Milky Way;
stars to the left, stars to the right,
yet the two of us can stay
shining or zoom into night.
We choose to pursue the blur:
it must be God or Love . . .
yes! it's female; we see Her!
it *is* God, blessed, from above,
emerging from a mist,
with angels' voices singing.
She brings what you have missed,
your tummy hungering.
We wake and see your mother's smiling eyes;
hers and yours being divine.
Her milk is St. Mary's milk, which will rise,
and make the bread and wine.

Felix Culpa*

In the beginning was the magic fall,
lucky Adam in Eden was guilty:
God provides bad mistakes for good of all

to learn from, when our backs are to the wall,
Second Adam our Saviour happily
in the beginning was the magic fall,

and She** taught us in Her St. Mark's*** to crawl
through problems and politics painfully:
God provides bad mistakes for good of all,

Our Mother** made tower of Babel tall
and most confusing linguistically:
in the beginning was the magic fall,

when over the waters as baptismal
She cleared up the screw-up spiritually
God provides bad mistakes for good of all,

God's Wind blew up flames Pentecostal,
all foreign tongues understood mutually:
in the beginning was the magic fall,
God provides bad mistakes for good of all.

---

*   'Lucky Mistake.' A villanelle based on the story of Adam's fall, the story of the tower of Babel—both in Genesis—and the account of Pentecost in Acts.

**   God is here conceived as feminine, as in Biblical and other sources.

***   A large Cathedral, in Minneapolis, where the vote took place that first allowed women into the Anglican priesthood.

Dismanteling Our Christmas Tree

Kenosis*

Down comes the big angel
Gabriel
from the very top
blowing his horn—
Christ is born.
Then a veritable crop
of lacey stars and snowflakes,
glass balls of silver and gold,
glass reindeer, German, delicate, old—
don't drop them for heaven sakes—
little angels, Santas, of felt and of wood,
items like circus seals with balls on noses—
no ancestor who bequeathed them would or could
explain their relevance, one supposes,
to Christmas. Dismantle the mantle: Wisemen, Kings,
baby Jesus; grandkids' stockings, now empty.
Lastly, take apart the tree,
after boxing all these things,
and fold its plastic limbs into a coffin-shaped container
as if embalmed until next year. It's a no-brainer
that I too have lost my topmost decoration
as well as, below that, much of my ornamentation
at age eighty-one; my limbs of flesh, not plastic, await inhumation
one day, or cremation, but my dismantling, while not embalmed,
will be by my faith becalmed,
and become a new creation,
beyond political liberation,
emptied of myself, emptied of things.

---

* A word referring to the Greek New Testament, where Jesus is said to have 'emptied' himself of equality with God.

Need a Meal

"Need a Meal," the sign said.
He held it up in front of my car,
but I drove on.
'I give him help through my church,'
I thought, 'I'm old too,' I thought:
"Yeah but I get three squares,
and a warm bed every day," I said aloud,
and he looked like he never slept,
except
under a bridge,
so bedraggled and cold. His ragged, mangled
clothes looked vaguely like U.S. Army.
"There aren't enough soup kitchens and shelters.
I have my 401K and a postal address.
I'll bet he's a vet,
with no family, with nothing,
but probably his service revolver
to swallow
if he can't get that meal,"
I thought, and made a u-turn.

Homage to Gerard Manley Hopkins*

Robert Sonkowsky, the poet, I'm to live a lot longer for writing?
playing with great grandchildren, nieces, nephews, great and grand?
So am I told, by the latest technology in my Doc's hand—
sudden reversal of earlier dire diagnosis so biting,

seemingly fatal and too soon to continue fighting,
hugging mortal broken mitral valve heart band
pulsing uneven beats as if not long for this land—
heart attacks galore here while out walking, no help within sighting.

Whereas my reprieve after all that has calmed my heart and fears,
my pen now takes its cues directly from my heart and its tears,
O God, I pray, from Your tears, and from poet Robert Sonkowsky,

You give me Your peace and Holy Comforter for many years
and enter the house of my heart so that my poetry clears,
my house that is Your house, for I give you forever its loving house key.

----

*   Sonnet in sprung and outriding rhythm, after Hopkins' Felix Randall:

FELIX RANDAL the farrier, O he is dead then? my duty all ended,
Who have watched his mould of man, big-boned and hardy-handsome
Pining, pining, till time when reason rambled in it and some
Fatal four disorders, fleshed there, all contended?

Sickness broke him. Impatient he cursed at first, but mended
Being anointed and all; though a heavenlier heart began some
Months earlier, since I had our sweet reprieve and ransom
Tendered to him. Ah well, God rest him all road ever he offended!

This seeing the sick endears them to us, us too it endears.
My tongue had taught thee comfort, touch had quenched thy tears,
Thy tears that touched my heart, child, Felix, poor Felix Randal;

How far from then forethought of, all thy more boisterous years,
When thou at the random grim forge, powerful amidst peers,
Didst fettle for the great grey drayhorse his bright and battering sandal!

Homage to John Ciardi*

I said to an ant on the wall,
"Hey, Dude, be careful, you'll fall!
    "You, said the ant,
    have a wrong-headed slant:
I'm not an ant, these aren't legs at all!
They're the tongs of an astronaut
on the moon!"—I said, "No they're not!"
    He said, "Not your call:
    the moon is a ball;
I dance on it and never get caught!"

---

*   He wrote many children's poems. The above is a modernistic imitation of the following:

   I said to a bug in the sink,
   "Are you taking a swim or a drink?"
   "I," said the bug
   "Am a sea-going tug.
   Am I headed for land, do you think?"
   "Don't be silly," I said. "That's no sea.
   It's a sink." "A sink it may be,
   But I'd sooner, I think,
   Be at sea in a sink,
   Than sink in the sea, sir," said he.

Waverly Songs II: Time, Timing, Change | 11

Great Grand Heritage

We are renewed!
We are new
great grandparents!
A little girl,
very little,
a premie,
one month early,
5 pounds, 3 ounces,
17 inches
long—
a string bean,
but a Queen!
Sing a Song
of joy!
Mom and Dad
had thought of a boy
but changed their minds
when they saw,
after five years of in vitro
with prayerful
seminal vesicle,
this miracle!

Lullaby*

Baby, Baby, you be peaceful, sweetly swaddled neck to toe,
Mama has been here to feed you; Daddy held you, voice so low.
Angels wings do now caress you; sleep now, Baby, not a peep.
God and Mom and Dad will bless you, if you let them go to sleep.

---

* Humorous, can be sung to the tune of Beethoven's "Hymn to Joy." After the author's great granddaughter came home from the hospital, she refused to sleep during the night and kept her parents awake most of the night. They put into her crib a musical toy that played Beethoven's hymn, which calmed her. So he composed a lullaby to that tune. Note the implication in line 4 that the baby has been keeping awake not only the parents, but also God!

A Haiku and a Poem in Rhymed Free Verse

Our drones overhead,
    suicide bombers below:
Whose side is God on?

Gun-Control Mostly Everywhere

We need guns
to keep out the huns,
and to prevent our own governments
from repressing us with violence.

Saigon Sonnet

The lights at home vary from halogen
to incandescent, to light-emitting diode,
to fluorescent, to fireplace, to candles, television.
These lamps, these flames, can remind you of a Pagoda,

but are never so bright as the light above men,
who forever returns to earth, and blazes, as Buddha,
or his priest, perishing in self-immolation,
protesting the murder of other Buddhists on the road

in Saigon—President Diem's attempt to purge
citizens not of the Roman Catholic belief—
Priests killing Priests, spreading grief
of War through the world in a universal dirge.

So much for the active peace and love of Christians!
So much for Buddhist passive non-violent resistance!

Gun Control, Almost Everywhere

Peaceful peoples need guns
to keep out the huns
and, with or without a second amendment,
or the equivalent,
to prevent
their own governments
from repressing them with violence.

March 5, 2013

[a rhyming tanka and haiku]

Today's newspaper spins
    the weather: snow to our chins,
storms, tornadic winds
    howling like violins.
    But what actually happens?

Little snow descends:
    not enough to slide rear-ends,
or cover our sins.

We Thank Our God for Moisture

We give thanks to God for moisture—for moisture and the sun,
water for every creature, sun on the beach for fun,
for light to think more clearly, for heat to warm the heart
toward neighbor and enemy—to Christ for a new start.

In the entire universe interplanetary
the Mother Earth is our nurse, and we will be wary,
protect against pollution, preserve God's creation,
and bring into fruition God's imagination.

The sun and moon with sun's wind, on earth cosmic wonders,
galactic holes where we've sinned, control our mood and blunders.
Our magnetic multiverse is coherent to God,
and leaves us humans no worse than subject to God's nod.

God's nod seems circumambient around about our earth,
but we know God's real intent, starting from the world's birth,
was beyond to boldly go to the boundless nothing,
where scientists do not know, nor preachers, anything.

Hail divine magnetism, hail! and let there be One,
holy Chrism, no schism, never under the Son,
the Logos, the planned Big Bang, away to Kingdom come,
while the maternal pain sang, to Christ's death never numb.

Boyhood Shoplifting
In the Sports Store
(Rhyming Tanka)

No one was watching
    that fishing knife: I snitched it,
into my pocket,
    blade up; as I walked away,
    it slashed my arm. Doc stitched it.

The Death of Little Nezzel [Free Verse]

They shot little Nezzel in the back
in his sleep at age five. They shot
many bullets driving by. They shot
through the walls into the living
room. They killed Nezzel sleeping
on the couch. His grandmother ran
outside screaming, clasping Nezzel's
photo to her breast, utter agony
on her face. The cops increase agony
and anger, think the killers known to
Nezzel's family. The usual black on black.
Nezzel's Mom said, "I want my baby back.
They took my hero. Are they happy now?"
Witnesses? Nezzel's Great Uncle
said he heard "boom, boom, boom"
and heard Nezzel cry out. A Vietnam veteran
saw several transients, who don't know who
saw what. No other evidence, apparently.
The cops merely appeal to the community
to come forth with information
and not attempt retaliation.
Earlier killings, also black on black.
See twitter.
They shot little Nezzel in the back
in his sleep at age five. They shot
many bullets driving by. Boom, boom
boom.

Luck, Be a Lady

Pagan *Felicitas* equals Christian grace
in blessed happiness and productivity,
but Eastern Christian St. Felicity*
gave birth to seven sons, martyred, the face
of each severed head she proudly displays
in a palm leaf right handily,
all in a row, all seven peacefully
sleepy statue-heads off their base,

faces previously anguished by tortured death,
grimace after grimace, like dice in a tray,
faces uniformly asleep as they lay,
baby eye-lids puffy from pain of the last breath.
St. Felicity is a deep legend
revealing inner horror of a religion.

---

*   Nothing is known of the actual, historical St. Felicity. The eastern church celebrates her seven legendary children's martyrdom on February 7.

My Hybrid Story

Thank God for global hybridization,
progressing, and mostly non-violent,
into which jihad, other hate, might dent
my politics, religion, Nation;

but I pray for ultimate elation
in the mystical body of Christ, sent
to parochial me, with glocal* bent,
namely, we are all one in Christ Risen!

The atoms that make up my molecules
share electrons with other entities,
which combine and receive duplicities,
good and bad, from heaven's revolving jewels.

My electrons imitate satellites,
timed by God particles** and chronome*** lights.

---

*   A portmanteau word consisting of "global" plus "local."

**   Mysterious but important, elementary particles whose definition is pursued by modern physicists. http://en.wikipedia.org/wiki/Higgs_boson

***   Chronomes are physiological entities described as "time structures," validated by statistics of measurements of such things as the effects of solar storms and interplanetary magnetism on our heart-rate, information collected globally, applied medically. http://www.ncbi.nlm.nih.gov/pubmed/10194568

Chronobiology*

The swirl of the galaxies seems clockwise,
the swirl of earth's oceans.
We swim intermittently in life,
with the current and against.

Our circles are welcoming or not;
our rhythms result in mystery,
gradually evolving God
merging into history.

---

*   The study of biological rhythms, or of the timing of intervals at which physiological events recur in animals and plants. This scientific field was founded by the author's friend, Franz Halberg, Professor of Physiology and Chronobiology. http://en.wikipedia.org/wiki/Franz_Halberg

A Play-World in a Driveway: Ave Maria

Their pretty three-year-old liked to play
on nice days in their own driveway:
she would either set up or roll
her toys on the smooth asphalt and crawl
or toddle on its dry, level surface and retrieve them.
Neighbors and passers by were delighted at the sight.
Since Daddy was at work all day,
she could sometimes leave them,
return later; so one day in her absence a limo with long, sleek hood
came down her street needing to turn around,
turned on the smooth asphalt driveway,
and crunch, crunch, crunch, inadvertently flattened
the take-apart airplane, princess guitar, and fairy castle,
not to mention that her sticker collection and wooden puzzle pieces
were scattered in the slip-stream. When she returned, bewildered, she stood,
she tried rescues, but cried for her Mother, ran back in the house—
Momma comforted her, helped recover and restore what they could.

Angels

I love the littlest angels,
those dancing on a pin point,
and I adore the huge motherly ones,
those so big you think their toes
alone might reach your nose
or go out of joint
and succumb to tons.

Feast from a Worker's Lunch Pail on a Hot
Summer's Day (Traditional Haiku)

Pita around beef,
    garlic pickles, and mustard.
Cold bottle of beer.

A-AHEM!

Ahem! A battle rages in my throat
when I inhale through my nose and exhale
through my larynx and mouth on the lowest note
my diaphragm and bass voice can avail.

The Valkyries enter the battlefield
like ravens, when I cough, and seek the best
dead warriors' souls to deliver sealed
unto Valhalla and Eternal Rest.

The rest are a post-nasal huck of phlegm,
the earthly end of my delightful life:
there'd been mistakes, there'd been sins to condemn
it was human, and it was full of strife.

So now when I clear my throat at surprises,
I inhale God's breath and my heart rises.

In Our Nation
And Everywhere
On Our Earth

O God,
may inspiration
from high office
and from poets laureate
not
become desperation
for immigration,
for opposition
to guns,
to further climate change,
and to murder,
by corporation,
of the poor,
and their emancipation,
or by my own
inaction.

Christ
(December 2012)

Christ is not in Christmas,
Christ is not in the glitz in the stores,
Christ is not in the ads on TV, on line, in print:
Christ is in the hands and feet of the Salvation Army bell-ringers,
Christ is in all those who give to the poor and tend to the sick,
Christ is in the tiny baby,
Christ is in the face of the baby's mother.

Persistence En Route

I did not receive an epiphany
en route to Damascus on some clear road:
slow maturing was my conversion mode,
illumined by God's gracious courtesy.

I groped, staggered, stumbled, and fell blindly
as I gradually grew up and rode
level awhile, until I could unload
my mistakes and sins temporarily.

Although I cannot escape from my guilt,
although I limp from my sciatic pain,
although mere confession, or spin, is vain,
still I want to live my life to the hilt:

I with my walker am running the race
where the finish line is God face-to-face.

Paratroopers, Skydivers, Balloonists [Sprung Rhythm]

Paratroopers' missions make them sober-faced;
skydivers and balloonists can be tourists and smile the while,
while they float through the air, surveying many a mile,
grassland and farmland in whatever patterns God has graced

placing the remainder of the original beauty, before in haste
seeking riches greedily we plundered the rest for vile
oil, for other sources of gold, not God, to pile
wealth like the Manhattan Towers: skydivers and balloonists, see the waste!

The image of the paratroopers of our Arsenal of Democracy*
is grim, but their Airborne spirit self-describes as "Crazy."
They bravely parachute behind enemy lines,

to hit from different angles and kill the enemy,
of course, not forgive, to preserve the lifestyle above, that we,
though non-Military, preserve in order to drink non-Eucharist fine wines.

---

* "Arsenal of Democracy" was a phrase coined by President F.D.R. in 1940 describing our
willingness to supply arms against the Nazis.

God's Kingdom
Is Here and Now
(Villanelle)

We sing we're free, God's love dispels the night
for all of us as one at break of day;
God's Grace is in us, surrounds us in light.

The diverse peoples rejoice at the sight
of the morning star, Tree of Life*, and say,
We sing we're free, God's love dispels the night!

Righteous people, beaten down by their fight
with evil, yet continue in God's way.
God's Grace is in us, surrounds us in light.

The river of the water of life, bright
as crystal, flows from God's throne—yes!—today!
We sing we're free, God's love dispels the night!

There is no need for lamp or sun: our light
is the Lord God, who sends evils away;
God's Grace is in us, surrounds us in light.

God's kisses, more than bread and wine, delight
us here on earth, more than we could pray!
We sing we're free, God's love dispels the night!
God's Grace is in us, surrounds us in light.

---

* A phrase of multiple meanings that connect different aspects of life and concepts into one.

Sprung Rhythm*

Our house has burned down.
It was struck by lightening.
Its dry timbers ignited.
We have no insurance.
Yet under black ashes
lives a dearest deep-down freshness.

---

*   More homage to G. M. Hopkins, alluding to his "The Grandeur of God."

Megan Ridgely
[double tanka]
Former Fitness Instructor, Waverly Gardens
Now Wellness Coordinator, Fort Dodge, Iowa
POETRY IN ACTION

Megan's Milwaukee
    verve: Barnstomp Blue-Grass "yeha!"
which rhymes with Yoga!
    she's poetry in action,
    that's my reaction:

water aerobics
    are her free verse and strophes,
not spilling a drop,
    though with a skip and a hop!
    She'll soon direct from the top!

become a farmer!
    grow organic vegetables,
fruits, herbs; and promote
    community supported
    organic agriculture,

while spoiling her cat,
    Nigel, black tabby, age four;
competing with her
    fraternal twin's and other
    four siblings' cats: let's party!

Megan's Milwaukee
    verve: Barnstomp Blue-Grass "yeha!"
which rhymes with Yoga!
    Her poetry, her life in action:
    I love her, not her picture.

Coochi Coo

When I roll over at night in bed
and reach my hand toward her head,
my fingers touch that softest skin
and stroke beneath her chin
along her neck, and her shoulder
rises to hug my hand, while I grow bolder.

A Twisted Brassiere Strap

A twisted brassiere strap
Imprints the shoulder
with an x.
A loosened brassiere strap
would be bolder
exposing a pap
and could lead to sex.

Our Times

LUV-i-dee DUV-i-dee,
serial intercourse.
Lovers extraordinaire
multiply sexed.

Idiocy rampantly,
Egomaniacly,
multiple marriages
multiply ex'd.

The Floozy

The floozy
under the awning
was a doozy,
    but of course I ignored
her wink, as if I was bored.
    Later, with a dawning,
        I kicked myself.

Hot Babe

Click, clack, clickety clack:
the sound of a hot babe
   in high heels . . .

International Red Hat Day*, April 25, 2013

Calling all ye proud olde bats!
Put on your red hats
with your garments of purple
defying old age, counting per pill,
with your younger pals, the gals in pink,
defying the fashionistas, making them blink!

---

*   The Red Hat Society states that its essence is summed up in the second line of Jenny
Joseph's poem "Warning:"

When I am an old woman I shall wear purple
With a red hat which doesn't go, and doesn't suit me.
And I shall spend my pension on brandy and summer gloves
And satin sandals, and say we've no money for butter.
I shall sit down on the pavement when I'm tired
And gobble up samples in shops and press alarm bells . . .
And run my stick along the public railings
And make up for the sobriety of my youth.
I shall go out in my slippers in the rain
And pick the flowers in other people's gardens
And learn to spit.
You can wear terrible shirts and grow more fat
And eat three pounds of sausages at a go
Or only bread and pickle for a week
And hoard pens and pencils and beermats and things in boxes.

But now we must have clothes that keep us dry
And pay out rent and not swear in the street
And set a good example for the children.
We must have friends to dinner and read the papers.

But maybe I ought to practice a little now?
So people who know me are not too shocked and surprised
When suddenly I am old and start to wear purple.

Ted's* for My Lymphedema

Pulling compression socks on to my feet
and up my legs makes me grunt, puff and bleat!
Moreover, as I dig my fingernails
into the stretchy cloth, it never fails
to tear them jagged and rip one bloody!

Then eight hours later I need my buddy,
my wife, to help and remove the damn things.
"Honey, bring me a beer! Pull these stockings."
And aah! She gets them off. My dearest wife.
That night I sleep with her, balm of my life.

---

*   A common brand name for compression stockings, worn to combat fluid-retention or varicose
      veins in feet, ankles, and legs.

The Syntax
of a Marriage

I complained to my father-in-law
of all people that his daughter
ought to stop finishing my sentences.
He paused, and said her mother has
the same habit with himself; women
talk faster than we men, never stop;
he stroked his chin, and added wisely,
"I guess we'll both have to finish our sentences."

To My Valentine

At age seventy-seven
on the way to heaven
I want you to know
that though
I may blow
my top at times of stress
over type-A business
and seem both sober and fierce,
I know I would die if anything would pierce
my heart by repelling your dearest sweetness
of tucking me in, keeping me from being sleepless.

Dream of the Rood*

I dreamt I talked with a telephone pole,
an orb, the sun, behind it, radiant;
its cross-arm and wires intertwined my soul;
galactic pulses, flashing, luminant.

Could crafted wood and metal enter hearts
estranged from Mother Earth's galacic beats?
Communicate with worms, with insect parts?
So many pathogens pollute her teats,

us human beings, and every animal
she nourishes to try to neutralize
the toxins, feeding food alchemical
to maggots, hugging bugs to sanitize.

My dream became a golden Celtic cross
embracing me and purging all my dross.

---

* "The Dream of the Rood" was one of the earliest Christian poems in Anglo-Saxon literature.
Rood is from Anglo-Saxon rod ('pole,' specifically 'crucifix,' as in the 10th century Vercelli Book
(a manuscript housed in a monastery in Italy), the poem may be one of the oldest works of
Old English literature. See http://en.wikipedia.org/wiki/The_Dream_of_the_Rood. The "orb" of
the Celtic Cross is the sun (Son), "the light of the world," as in "St. Patrick's Breastplate, the
Irish melody of the Christian hymn "I bind myself unto the Name of the Trinity," intertwining
God with all creation, including all the animals.
Both the Celtic Cross and the alchemists aimed to sublimate to the perfection of gold.

Moses Parted the Red Sea [sonnet]

Moses parted the Red Sea: Israel with ease
walked through; God drowned Pharaoh's men, horse and all,
lining the shore with Egyptian bodies,
over which Israel gloats, triumphs, stands tall.

Moses and his men celebrate with song,
and his sister Miriam with castanet
leads glorying women to dance along,
sings 'horse and rider no longer a threat.'

We Christians, of course, insist God is Love
and turn the other cheek, so mild and meek
our drones alone kill more kids from above
per bomb than Texas kills killers per week!

Chariots and lances, bows and arrows,
guns and bombs are God's creation, He knows.

Barbara's Rainbow
(a truncated sonnet*)

When I came home, she was not on the couch:
my wife was sitting half-sprawled on the floor,
above her left eye a goose egg, a huge pouch;
her wet bare feet had slipped, both knees were sore;

she'd returned from swimming, removed wet shoes,
the laminated floor had caused the fall.
We iced her lump, but next day reds and blues,
yellows, greens masked her eyes as for the ball

at Marti Gras. To her mirror she said,
"I look like a prize fighter who has lost
the fight." Her doctor examined her head,
pronounced her fit, but pressed a spot: Barb tossed

an "Ouch!"

---

* In a truncated sonnet, instead of the final two lines, the final two words rhyme with the first line ("couch" and "ouch"). See Trellis Magazine www.trellismagazine.com/files/Trellis_Issue_12.pdf

The Screaming Siren

I'd been asleep in my chair
    in the Emergency Room lobby
waiting for news of my wife—

    shocking lights through the window:
red, green, yellow, residual purple on steel.

    I saw strange-looking people in the lobby;
when my medical son came wheeling
    my thank-God-ok wife, his mother,
he explained these were bipolar people
    and criminal gang members:
hence the presence of the Ramsey County Sheriff
    and other kind and loving hospital staff.

Blessings
[sonnet]

A blessing is the opposite of a curse.
If we are a blessing to each other,
this means we give the love we got at birth
from embracing mothers, sisters, brothers—

blessings people need to give and receive,
to support, nourish, love one another;
no heart lacks this divine need; intimacy,
when welcomed, enlivens; rejected, smothers.

May God, our Creator, lift us beyond—
may Christ, God's Son-in-our-image, bless all—
may the Holy Spirit comfort and bind
us into One World, with never a wall

between American patriotism
and any other nation's pacifism.

Peonies

My mom called them Pinees.
Pink ones proliferate here in profusion.
Their fragrance,
I'm sure, rises to heaven,
like incense,
and my mom finds it pretty pleasant.

For Stella Marie Petersen

(a sonnet)

Beloved husband, Pete, the pilot, thrived
on the well-being of community;
American poet Phoebe Carey
wrote "The Leak in the Dike, therein contrived

the brave little boy Peter, who arrived,
acted just in time to save his country,
stuck his finger in the hole still tiny
before it burst and none would have survived.

For Stella this story is metaphor—
little boy Peter is inside big Pete,
whose spirit holds back waters of defeat
in times of grief this side of Heaven's door.

Pete's sweetness flies above in his airplane,
his finger protecting, soothing her pain.

At Age Seventy-Seven

At age seventy-seven
I miss my mother more
even than when she
died, and my wife
compensates
in both roles more
and more than I
deserve or can
reciprocate.
Now and at the hour
of my death
I fear being lost
as dust in wind
or earth.

Color Blind Tanka

My wife says her robe
is puce, but I say purple;
purple is not named
exotically from charts
in Sears Roebuck catalogues.

At Age Seventy-Eight in Bed

I struggled to remember the phone number
of my oldest and best buddy,
couldn't just couldn't remember,
tried memorokinetic motion of dialing,
didn't help.

Tried another friend,
a girl friend,
still couldn't couldn't find
either number in phone books,
paged and paged,
using my magnifying glass,
but remembered them clearly
smiling beckoning,
couldn't couldn't couldn't,

then remembered they're both dead.

Just a dream, just a dream.

I Wonder

I wonder how my childhood home looks now.
Dilapidated? Bent and gray, like me?
Inside do wooden floorboards creakily
re-echo ghostly footsteps remembering how
my Dad and Mom would walk from room to room,
my little brother toddled everywhere,
his lighter treads yet registering his pair
of baby shoes, while I would thump and zoom?

Outside does sun still shine or snow still fall
on sidewalks, bushes, flowers, trees, and lawn?
Do kids still play around there? Are they gone?
I must go home, the very house, to know
by knocking on the door and pleading for
a tour of floors to stave my thirst for more.

The Giraffe and the Monkey

The giraffe—so many bones—nibbles and stumbles,
tearing spider webs, nipping tendrils
highest up, his legs like pencils
poke holes beneath till the turf crumbles;
his majestic speechless swaying humbles
insects under hooves as if pursued by devils,
but not the chattering monkey in her revels,
as she brandishes a banana and never fumbles.

Taoist Tanka

May I be gentle
    as a baby's hands held high
in sleep and as strong
    as when she seems to conduct
    symphonies, and will one day.

Lizzi's Hands
(A Villanelle)

"As the sun was setting, all those who had any who were sick with various kinds of diseases brought them to him; and he laid his hands on each of them and cured them." Luke 4:40 NRSV

Lizzi's hands are holy: they help, they heal
young and old, those who seek her therapy,
the earth, her dogs, her patients, all who feel—

she gives them her hands, her hugs, with much zeal;
digs gardens as her knowing eyes decree.
Lizzi's hands are holy: they help, they heal.

Her eyes are blue with that steady appeal:
centered, she looks at me and centers me,
the earth, her dogs, her patients, all who feel

her hands, her spirit: chrism of her seal
on our heads, firming our identity.
Lizzi's hands are holy: they help, they heal

us all, they sew, make crafts, make us be real
and in love with all of one family,
the earth, her dogs, her patients, all who feel:

from her garden she presents the best meal
a communicant gets eternally.
Lizzi's hands are holy: they help, they heal
the earth, her dogs, her patients, all who feel.

LIZZI Tanka

Lizzi prescribed hugs,
    for my sanity, she said—
her most precious gift—
    it went to my heart and head:
    I preach it, gospel for all.

Stand-By Lights

I have hugged many a tree,
at least virtually,
supplicating them to remember me
in their relative longevity.
My TV, CD and DVD players,
and their speakers,
my computer and its printers
have stand-by lights,
like eyes,
that stay on days and nights
and will stay on after mine
are closed.